Sleuth
ReadyGEN™

PEARSON

Glenview, Illinois
Boston, Massachusetts
Chandler, Arizona
Hoboken, New Jersey

ISBN-13: 978-0-328-81947-8
ISBN-10: 0-328-81947-6
9 16

Contents

Unit 4 Exploring New Worlds

From: The Super Sleuths

Subject: Mysteries

Dear Sleuthhound,

It's up to you! We need your help to gather the evidence, follow the clues, and solve some big questions. You will have to use all your sleuth skills and tools. There are lots of mysteries in the pages of this book. You will need to be curious and ask interesting questions. Use the evidence and clues you discover to explain your thinking to others. As you unlock mysteries from places near and far, keep practicing these Super Sleuth Steps along the way!

Good luck!

SUPER SLEUTH STEPS

Gather Evidence

- Look back through the text and the images to find clues and evidence others might have missed.

- Record and organize the evidence. How do the pieces fit together? Is there a sequence? Did one event cause another?

Ask Questions

- A great question is one that nobody else may think to ask. Be prepared to learn something amazing!

- Ask about something that interests you. Curiosity is the most important trait of a Super Sleuth.

Make Your Case

- Look at all the evidence and clues. What conclusion can you make? Take a stand!

- A convincing argument includes a clearly stated position or conclusion, is based on solid evidence, and is presented with confidence. Be convincing!

Prove It!

- It's time to wrap up the case. Are you ready to show what you learned? Amaze your audience!

- Work to put all the pieces together whether you work alone or as part of a team. Every team member should have a voice.

Unit 1
Depending on Each Other

Hello, Sleuthhounds!

In this unit, you will be looking for clues and evidence. Here are some sleuth tips to help you. Get ready to take the challenge!

Sleuth Tips

Gather Evidence

Where do sleuths find evidence?

- Sleuths find clues in the text. They use background knowledge or their own experiences as well.
- Sleuths hunt for clues in images. They study data on charts and graphs. They read captions and headings.

Ask Questions

What types of questions do sleuths ask?

- Good sleuths ask questions to find out who, what, when, where, why, and how.
- Sleuths ask about the big picture as well as the details. They ask questions that will help them gather evidence.

Make Your Case

How do sleuths reach a conclusion?

- Sleuths look at the facts they have gathered. Sleuths figure out what conclusion they can draw from the evidence.
- Sleuths know that a strong case is supported by information that is based on facts, not opinions.

Prove It!

How do sleuths prove they have learned something new?

- Sleuths think about what they learned on their own and from others, as well as from asking more questions.
- Sleuths organize the information so that it is presented clearly.

Fishy Business!

The Columbia River flows westward for more than 1,200 miles (1,931 kilometers) across the Northwest. A paradise for fish, right? At one time, it was. Yet when humans decided to control the water rushing to the ocean, no one asked the fish what they thought.

A dam is a man-made structure built across a river. Dams both help prevent flooding and provide water for irrigation. Larger dams generate pollution-free and inexpensive hydroelectric power. Over time, more than four hundred dams have been built along the Columbia River, eleven of which extend completely across the river.

Consider, however, how these dams affect the natural environment, specifically the salmon living in these waters. Salmon make only two long journeys during their lives. Hatched in rivers far from the ocean, young salmon swim to the ocean where they spend their adult lives. Near the end of their lives, they swim back to their birthplace. In the cool streams, females lay eggs, and males fertilize them.

What happens when a young fish swimming toward the ocean encounters a dam that crosses the entire river? Water stored behind the dam rushes downward through chutes and turns huge turbines to generate electricity. Spinning blades are not a healthy environment for fish!

If the fish somehow makes it to the ocean, it must eventually swim upstream against the current to reach its spawning ground. Fish can do this for long distances when the slope is gentle. However, climbing a dam more than 100 feet (30 meters) high is quite a challenge! Because dams make it difficult for fish to spawn, salmon and trout populations along the Columbia River have dropped from 16 million to 2.5 million.

Since the 1930s, builders have added "fishways" such as fish ladders to dams. A fish ladder is a series of gradually ascending pools next to a dam that are filled with rushing water. The fish swim upriver against the current, leaping from a lower pool to a higher one. They rest in the pool before repeating the process until they are above the dam.

Fish ladders and other structures are like elevators. They fill with fish, rise to the top of the dam, and open to let the fish out. They can add millions of dollars to a dam's cost, but isn't the expense worth it? Causing whole populations of fish to die out is unthinkable. Preserving the environment is priceless.

Sleuth Work

Gather Evidence
List three ways that dams in the Northwest have helped residents of the area.

Ask Questions What are three questions about salmon near the Columbia River that are not answered in the text or by the images?

Make Your Case How well does the writer use details to describe the structures built to help the fish? Use examples from the text to explain your answer.

Welcome to the Neighborhood?

Today more and more people live in homes built where wildlife once roamed freely. Some folks enjoy their animal neighbors. For example, they like watching deer or birds in their backyard. Others view the animals as intruders—unwelcome and annoying. Either way, the fact is that humans are increasingly moving into animal territory. Because interactions between people and wild animals can't be completely avoided, humans must be willing to change some of their habits.

Take birds, for example. They're often attracted to the brilliant lights of city skyscrapers, but the lights can disrupt the birds' migration patterns. Some become exhausted and confused, repeatedly circling the buildings. As a result, the birds fall behind schedule. This increases the likelihood that they won't survive winter storms before reaching their destination. Some cities, such as Chicago, have started voluntary Lights Out programs. Buildings dim or turn off their lights between 11 P.M. and sunrise during the migration season.

Lights on beaches affect wildlife too. Newly hatched sea turtles wait below the sand until dark. Then, instinct and the brightness of the horizon over the water lead them to the sea. If they see lights on the beach, the hatchlings may move toward

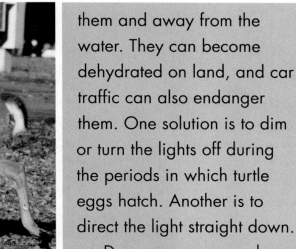

them and away from the water. They can become dehydrated on land, and car traffic can also endanger them. One solution is to dim or turn the lights off during the periods in which turtle eggs hatch. Another is to direct the light straight down.

Deer, opossums, and raccoons can do serious damage to gardens and homes. Deer will eat a wide variety of plants, but a fence or bright, motion-activated lights may keep them away. By trimming tree branches, homeowners can prevent opossums and raccoons from jumping onto a roof and, from there, entering an attic or a chimney. An effective way to discourage raccoons, as well as coyotes and red foxes, is to keep garbage cans tightly closed. Also, people shouldn't leave food outside for their pets. It may attract wildlife. Even an open bird feeder may attract more than birds.

Some people support trapping and relocating unwanted animals, but these actions are often ineffective. Studies show that more than half of the animals that are relocated won't survive in a new place. Nobody says it will always be easy, but learning how to live side-by-side with wild animals might be a better solution.

Sleuth Work

Gather Evidence List key details in two columns, one for problems wild animals can cause for humans and the other for problems humans can cause for animals.

Ask Questions What questions about bird migration or the Lights Out program do you have after reading this article?

Make Your Case Does this writer express a point of view on living among animals? Cite details from the text to explain your thinking.

The BIG Move

Ever since Hannah was an infant, she and her parents had left their tiny city apartment and spent two weeks in the country every June. They rented a big old farmhouse on a large farm. Though the farm was no longer in use, there were acres of fields and woods to explore and even a pond for swimming. Hannah considered those two weeks at the farm the best two weeks of the year.

This June, like every other, everyone packed swimsuits, shorts, and hiking shoes and eagerly headed to the country. Hannah could tell something was different, though, because her mom and dad grew especially quiet as they approached the farm. Hannah figured out why when she saw the big FOR SALE sign posted at the end of the gravel driveway. "The owners are selling the farm! What will we do next June?" Hannah exclaimed.

"How would you feel about living in the farmhouse all year?" Hannah's dad asked. At first, Hannah thought to herself that it sounded fantastic, but then she wasn't so sure. She had lots of questions: *How could she make new friends in the country? Where would she go to school? What do people do for fun in the winter? Could she keep taking karate lessons like she did in the city?*

Hannah's parents tried to reassure her. She would adapt quickly, they explained. Hannah could have friends visit from the city, and she would certainly be able to keep studying karate. Her parents told her they would move before the school year began so that Hannah would have an easier time adjusting. By the end of the week, the decision was finalized. For the next two months, Hannah tried to stay positive. But she also made herself a list of all the things she would miss about city life—like the bright lights at night and all the stores, restaurants, and museums.

When moving day came, Hannah was both excited and nervous—just like her parents. During the first week of school, she made a new friend. Soon the girls started riding their bikes together, and they registered for the same karate class. Hannah even started to enjoy the quietness of the country. It certainly was not as exciting and busy as the city, but the farm was lovely, and the woods were filled with adventures. She could still visit the bright lights and excitement of the big city. Best of all, living in the country versus a small, cramped apartment in the city gave her the best opportunity of all— her family adopted a puppy!

Sleuth Work

Gather Evidence Identify three elements of city life that Hannah thinks she will miss before she moves and three elements of country life that she enjoys after the move.

Ask Questions When Hannah thinks about moving to the country, she has a lot of questions about the move. List three more questions you would have if you were to move to a new place.

Make Your Case What do you think is the most convincing evidence that shows Hannah's feelings changed about the move?

the Tree of HEAVEN

"California, the most wonderful place on the Earth!" sang my father as we trudged through the streets of San Francisco.

I made a face. I had been in California for just a few hours, but already I was terribly homesick for our village in China.

"Here in California," my mother explained to me, "there is wealth everywhere and plenty of jobs to be had."

My father had been to America twice before, without us. He had gotten work in factories and on the railroad. He had saved his earnings. Now our whole family had journeyed across the Pacific to begin our new life in a new land.

"You will like it here, Mei Li," added my mother.

I had lived in our village my whole life—all of ten years. How could I live without our little river, the rice fields, the beautiful Tree of Heaven outside our window? I had not seen a single Tree of Heaven in San Francisco.

"Life is better in America," my father explained as we crossed the dusty street. "China has wars and floods and famines, but such disasters are almost unknown in California."

Perhaps, I thought, but California was crowded, with strange people everywhere, people with too-pale skin and too-light hair, people who jabbered in a language I did not know. The houses looked uninviting, the air smelled different, and how, I wondered, could I ever feel at home here?

"That blue house," said my father, pointing, "is where I lived when I worked in the fish factory seven years ago. It will be our

house now that we are immigrants in this land. It can never be the same as our house in China, but we will make it a home."

At first I looked at the house and frowned. Then I noticed something. A tree that I knew well stood outside the blue house. "A Tree of Heaven!" I cried, running to touch the familiar branches.

"A Tree of Heaven at our new home," my father replied. "Seven years ago I took a seed from our Tree of Heaven in China, brought it across the ocean, and planted it here. I know how much you love that tree, Mei Li," he told me, his soft voice quivering. "This house could not be our home without a Tree of Heaven outside."

I breathed in the scent of the leaves, happier than I had been in weeks. "Thank you, Father," I murmured. I walked up to the house and opened the door to our new life.

Sleuth Work

Gather Evidence What details reveal Mei Li's opinion of California? List at least two similarities or differences between her opinion and the opinions of her parents.

Ask Questions After reading the story, what do you still wonder about? Ask three questions you have about what happened to Mei Li and her family.

Make Your Case The writer carefully selected words to describe California. How do the descriptions change depending on who is describing the state?

Unit 2
Finding Courage

Hey there, Sleuthhounds!

In this unit, you will be looking for clues about courageous people. Here are some sleuth tips to help you. Get to it!

Sleuth Tips

Gather Evidence

Why do sleuths reread?

- Sleuths realize that they may miss details when they first read something.
- Sleuths search for new details when they reread. They're always on the hunt!

Ask Questions

What makes a great question?

- Sleuths ask clear and focused questions that will help them learn something or find more clues.
- When sleuths ask great questions, it helps other sleuths think more critically.

Make Your Case

How do sleuths make a clear case?

- Sleuths stick to the point. They show what they know. They open and close the case with a clear statement.
- Sleuths provide support for their reasons. The reasons they present are logical and in the proper sequence.

Prove It!

What do sleuths do when they work with other sleuths?

- Sleuths believe in teamwork. They share the facts they have learned.
- Sleuths know that working together can be hard work but also lots of fun!

THE PRICE OF FREEDOM

Harriet Tubman

What are you worth? If you were enslaved in the United States in 1850, you were a possession. Slave owners could buy and sell you for as much as $3,000. For this reason, slave owners offered rewards for the capture of enslaved people who had escaped.

The Underground Railroad was a secret network of people who believed that slavery was wrong. They risked the consequences of breaking the law to help people escape slavery and make their way to northern states or Canada where slavery was outlawed. The use of railroad terms helped ensure secrecy. Routes between *stations*—homes of sympathetic families who would feed and hide the enslaved people— were called *lines*. *Conductors* guided runaways from one station to another. Fugitives were referred to as *packages* or *freight*.

Those people who contributed to the Underground Railroad included free African Americans and sympathetic whites. However, one of the best-known conductors had escaped slavery herself. Harriet Tubman was born enslaved in Maryland around 1820. By the fall of 1849, Tubman made the decision to flee. If she couldn't have freedom, she would prefer death. A friendly white neighbor told her how to find the first safe house on her path to freedom. When she finally reached the North, where slavery was outlawed, Harriet said, "I had crossed the line. I was free; but there was no one to welcome me to the land of freedom. I was a stranger in a strange land."

Harriet's goal became to help those she had left behind, including her family members. Rather than simply enjoying her newly found freedom, she got a job in Philadelphia and saved her money.In 1850, Harriet returned to Maryland and started leading her family to freedom. Over the next ten years, she made the hazardous trip south and back numerous times. Because of Harriet's efforts, her family and around seventy other enslaved people escaped slavery. She never "lost" a fugitive. She never allowed anyone to give up. Harriet was so determined to see these people reach freedom that she carried a gun to threaten the fugitives if they became too tired or decided to turn back. When a person's resolve wavered, she advised, "You'll be free or die."

One newspaper in Maryland offered a $100 reward for her capture. But to the scores of people Harriet Tubman helped to reach freedom, she was priceless!

Routes of the Underground Railroad

SLEUTH WORK

Gather Evidence What clues can you find that explain why Harriet was willing to risk her own freedom to help enslaved people escape?

Ask Questions After reading the text, what more would you like to know about slavery and the Underground Railroad? Ask two questions you are curious about.

Make Your Case Which of the visual elements that accompany this selection do you think is most helpful? Explain your reasons.

ON LOYALTY TO COUNTRY

BY SARAH WILSON

Yesterday I walked the historic Freedom Trail in Boston. The Trail starts at the oldest park in the country, Boston Common, where British soldiers camped before the Revolutionary War. It ends at Bunker Hill, the site of the first major battle. The American Patriots worked hard for independence from England. Seeing Benjamin Franklin's statue, Paul Revere's house, and Faneuil Hall made me proud to be an American. Franklin was a political leader and signer of the Declaration of Independence. Revere made a legendary midnight ride to warn that the British were coming by sea. At Faneuil Hall, Samuel Adams gave speeches to inspire the colonists.

However, the Freedom Trail honors only those who worked for independence. My ancestors came from Great Britain in 1774. While they appreciated the opportunities they had in the colonies, they were also extremely proud of their home country. They remained loyal to England during the American Revolution. The rebels criticized them for being traitors, but the Loyalists believed they were right for being loyal to their ruler, King George III. Even William Franklin, Ben Franklin's son, supported England. He was a respected governor of New Jersey. Disagreement over patriotic loyalties resulted in a lifetime rift between the two men.

Loyalists believed a government that worked should not be replaced. Moreover, they felt the taxes they paid the British government were not extreme. They felt that those who protested were upset because they had not paid the taxes before. Some who wanted freedom from Great Britain believed the colonies did not have enough say in the decisions of Parliament. Yet, Loyalists argued, each colony had a governor who could send a representative to Great Britain to speak before Parliament.

Some questioned the rebels' tactics. For one, Adams wrote letters to newspapers signed with different names. He wanted to make it seem that everyone in the colonies desired independence. In fact, many colonists had not made up their minds about independence at the time war broke out.

For these reasons, I propose that a statue be commissioned to represent a hero who fought on the side of Great Britain. One consideration could be Patrick Ferguson, who was an officer in the British Army. At the Battle of Brandywine in 1777, he acted with honor. He had an opportunity to shoot a rebel officer and did not. He later wrote that the thought of shooting someone in the back "disgusted" him. Some stories suggest that the rebel officer may have been George Washington!

SLEUTH WORK

Gather Evidence Find at least three key points of disagreement between the Patriots and the Loyalists about independence for the colonies.

Ask Questions After reading the text, what are two questions you would ask about Loyalists?

Make Your Case What was a challenge faced by Loyalists during the American Revolution? How might the writer have described the challenge more vividly?

Bound for Kansas!

Jefferson Wilson was born into slavery in the South. The North's victory in the Civil War had promised opportunities for a better life, but the realities had fallen far short of what he expected. For all intents and purposes, as sharecroppers, Wilson and other former slaves were not truly free. No wonder they were dissatisfied with life in their Tennessee town.

A white man owned the land that Jefferson Wilson, his wife, and his three sons worked. The rent was so high and the rates for crops so low that his family was constantly in debt. The same was true for all sharecroppers. Living conditions were harsh, and racial tensions made Wilson worry for the safety of his family.

One day as he walked through Nashville, Jefferson Wilson spotted an advertisement for homesteading in Kansas. An acquaintance of his, businessman Benjamin Singleton, had posted it. Wilson investigated further and soon realized that he could afford transportation for his family if he didn't buy seeds for another year of sharecropping. After long discussions with friends and family—many of whom chose to stay in Tennessee—the Wilsons decided to head west with Mr. Singleton and one other family to help establish the all-black community of Dunlap, Kansas. The journey was long and difficult, with yellow fever claiming the lives of several travelers. Hopes of finding new opportunities sustained the pioneers.

Original advertisement encouraging homesteading in Kansas

Ho for Kansas!

Brethren, Friends, & Fellow Citizens:

I feel thankful to inform you that the

REAL ESTATE

AND

Homestead Association,

Will Leave Here the

15th of April, 1878,

In pursuit of Homes in the Southwestern Lands of America, at Transportation Rates, cheaper than ever was known before.

For full information inquire of

Benj. Singleton, better known as old Pap,

NO. 5 NORTH FRONT STREET.

Beware of Speculators and Adventurers, as it is a dangerous thing to fall in their hands.

Nashville, Tenn., March 18, 1878.

Early Kansas homesteaders

When the Wilsons arrived, they faced many physical and emotional challenges. Farming the Kansas land proved difficult, and they were lonely. But one thing made all the difference—Jefferson Wilson and his neighbors owned the land they worked and the houses they built. It was theirs. Though they experienced some discrimination in Kansas, they no longer lived in constant fear for their lives.

The community established its own school—The Dunlap Academy and Mission School—which Wilson was proud to say his sons attended. As time passed, more and more people came to Dunlap, creating a tight-knit community of hundreds of black families.

Despite the difficulties of constructing their sod house and clearing ground to plant, Jefferson Wilson and his wife never regretted their decision to begin a new life in Kansas. Eventually, their crops prospered, and life became easier. They had sacrificed a lot to start over, but they knew they had made the right choice for their family. Most importantly, they finally knew what freedom truly meant.

Sleuth Work

Gather Evidence What motivated Jefferson Wilson to leave Tennessee for Kansas? List at least three clues from the story that help explain why he moved.

Ask Questions List three questions you would like to ask Jefferson Wilson or his family about their first year living in Dunlap, Kansas.

Make Your Case How does understanding the time period after the Civil War help you to better understand the actions of Jefferson Wilson?

A Voice for Women

In 1815, when Elizabeth Cady Stanton was born in Johnstown, New York, males had much more influence and many more options for employment than females in the United States. American women could not become government leaders, preachers, or professors. Girls with an interest in public speaking or politics were steered in other directions. The law even barred women from voting. Like other girls of her time, Elizabeth was expected to become a wife and mother when she grew up—and not much else.

It's not surprising that Elizabeth Cady Stanton eventually became a wife and mother. Though she loved her family, Stanton was passionate about politics as well. One of her causes was the effort to abolish slavery in the United States. Before her marriage in 1840, moreover, she had made supporting this movement a priority. Following her marriage, she and her husband attended an antislavery conference in England.

Stanton's main concern, though, was fair treatment for women. In the mid-1800s, the laws recognized few rights of American women. Besides being barred from voting, women could not serve on juries and were denied an equal education. Women could not divorce their husbands. In 1848, Stanton helped organize the Women's Rights Convention in Seneca Falls, New York. She wrote a declaration of women's rights, which was passed by the convention's delegates. This document demanded that the same rights be recognized for women as for men.

By the 1860s, Stanton was speaking and writing frequently about women's rights. Many Americans—men and women alike—

disagreed with her positions. Some mocked her, while others simply ignored her. Standing strong in her beliefs, Stanton continued to travel extensively, making speeches and trying to change people's minds.

Stanton had disagreements with people on her side too. After the Civil War, which ended slavery in 1865, most women's rights advocates supported granting voting rights to African Americans. Yet, when politicians decided to allow black men to vote—while continuing to keep women of all races from voting—Stanton became furious, adamantly refusing to support voting rights for African American men if women could not vote. Many other women's rights activists, however, disagreed with her. The result was a split; from 1869 to 1890, the women's rights movement formed two competing organizations.

Fighting for women's rights into her old age, Stanton inspired thousands of Americans. Though she died in 1902, eighteen years later the United States approved the Nineteenth Amendment, which at last recognized women's right to vote.

Sleuth Work

Gather Evidence Identify at least three of Elizabeth Cady Stanton's main complaints about the legal status of women in the 1800s.

Ask Questions Suppose you could travel back to the 1800s. List two questions you would ask Stanton's supporters and two to ask of her opponents. Tell why you chose these questions.

Make Your Case Why does the time period of this selection make a difference in your understanding of Elizabeth Cady Stanton's actions? Use details from the text in your answer.

Unit 3
Understanding the Universe

Hello there, Sleuthhounds!

In this unit, you will be looking for clues about looking beyond what we see each day. Here are some sleuth tips to help you. Be creative!

Sleuth Tips

Gather Evidence

How do sleuths get clues from images?

- Sleuths know that clues can be hidden in images. They look closely at pictures, charts, maps, and other visuals.
- Sleuths make connections between text and images and other visuals. These connections may lead to new clues!

Ask Questions

Why are sleuths so curious?

- Sleuths know that questions and answers go together. They need one to get the other.
- Sleuths love surprises. They are excited to follow hints and clues that lead them to answers or more questions.

Make Your Case

Why don't all sleuths agree on the answers?

- Sleuths don't all work the same way. They may find different things and may put things together differently.
- Sleuths know we all have had different experiences. These differences may result in conclusions that aren't quite the same.

Prove It!

How can sleuths be creative when showing what they have learned?

- Super sleuths explain their ideas using descriptive words and images to paint a clearer picture for others.
- Sleuths know the power of persuasive language. They use robust words to capture their audience's attention.

TECHNOLOGY and TREASURE

Historians estimate that about three million shipwrecks lie on the ocean floor. Many contain gold, silver, or precious gems. Why not grab a snorkel and fins, take a few diving lessons, and head into the ocean to find a treasure? Unfortunately, it's not that simple. Famous treasure hunter Mel Fisher and his crew spent sixteen years searching for the wreck of the seventeenth-century Spanish ship *Atocha* (ah-TOE-chah) before locating it in 1985.

High-tech electronic equipment has made the task of finding underwater treasure—like the more than 100,000 silver coins found in the *Atocha*—a lot easier than it once was. Consider the steps that many modern treasure hunters take.

FIND THE WRECK Sonar devices towed behind ships send out sound waves, which bounce off the ocean floor and back to the ship. A computer creates a three-dimensional map that can be used to locate hidden wrecks. Even ships completely covered by sand can be detected.

GET TO THE WRECK Divers use SCUBA (**S**elf-**C**ontained **U**nderwater **B**reathing **A**pparatus) gear to explore wrecks in shallow water. The diver, breathing a mixture of gases held in tanks, carries a light, safety equipment, and tools. In deep water, searchers operate sophisticated robotic devices, including **R**emotely **O**perated **V**ehicles (ROVs).

LOCATE BURIED OBJECTS Sand shifts with ocean currents, so divers may use submersible detectors to locate metals below the ocean floor. Other devices similar to leaf blowers move sand and sediment away from objects. Reversing the flow of air can vacuum small items directly up to the recovery ship.

MAP THE SITE Divers use powerful lights and high-definition cameras to take thousands of photographs. These are assembled into a detailed map of the wreck.

RECOVER OBJECTS Crews on recovery ships lower baskets to bring up small objects. Cranes or robotic arms move larger items. The water dredge is another useful excavation tool. With a long tube, it functions much like an underwater vacuum cleaner.

CONSERVE ARTIFACTS Objects exposed to seawater for centuries are often covered with minerals. Conservation experts use everything from dental picks to air-powered chisels to expose the treasure underneath the crust.

All this technology is not cheap. Mel Fisher spent more than $58 million in his search for the *Atocha*. Is it worth it? Many marine treasure hunters think so. Like a buried time capsule, shipwrecks may hold valuable treasures and also provide a fascinating window into the past.

SLEUTH WORK

Gather Evidence Why did the author write this selection? List three clues that help you understand the author's purpose.

Ask Questions What questions about the *Atocha* shipwreck or Mel Fisher's discovery of its treasure would you be interested in researching? Where would you look to learn more about the subject?

Make Your Case List some of the scientific vocabulary used in this selection. Choose one of the terms and write a definition for it from a dictionary.

Divers searching and blowing the sand on the sea floor

Careers in the Space Industry

Do you like gazing at the stars on a clear night? Are you fascinated by the enormity of the universe? Do you wonder if there is life "out there"? Perhaps a career in the space industry is for you. Most of the job opportunities in space exploration or research involve science and math, but writers and artists also play a role in this exciting field.

The most common career involving space is astronomy. Astronomers use science to study the universe. These men and women study the motions, positions, sizes, and makeup of heavenly bodies, such as stars, planets, and galaxies. Astronomers often get their doctoral degrees. Their jobs might involve teaching at a university, doing research about how something in space works, or using enormous telescopes and supercomputers to analyze how objects in space move.

Some astronomers specialize in astrophysics. That is, they study the physical and chemical measurements of heavenly bodies. The astrophysicists at the National Aeronautics and Space Administration (NASA) focus on answering three main questions: How does the universe work? How did we get here? Are we alone? These specialists use their knowledge of physics, along with advanced technology, to continue to search for answers to these questions.

If this kind of science isn't up your alley, you might be interested in another career in the space industry— engineering. Electrical engineers are responsible for designing rocket engines, propulsion devices, and satellites. They focus on the way these things will function outside Earth's atmosphere. Mechanical engineers work on any moving parts of a spacecraft, from radios to robots. They, too, have to think about the way the space environment will affect materials. Finally, software engineers program the computers that run the spacecraft that electrical and mechanical engineers design.

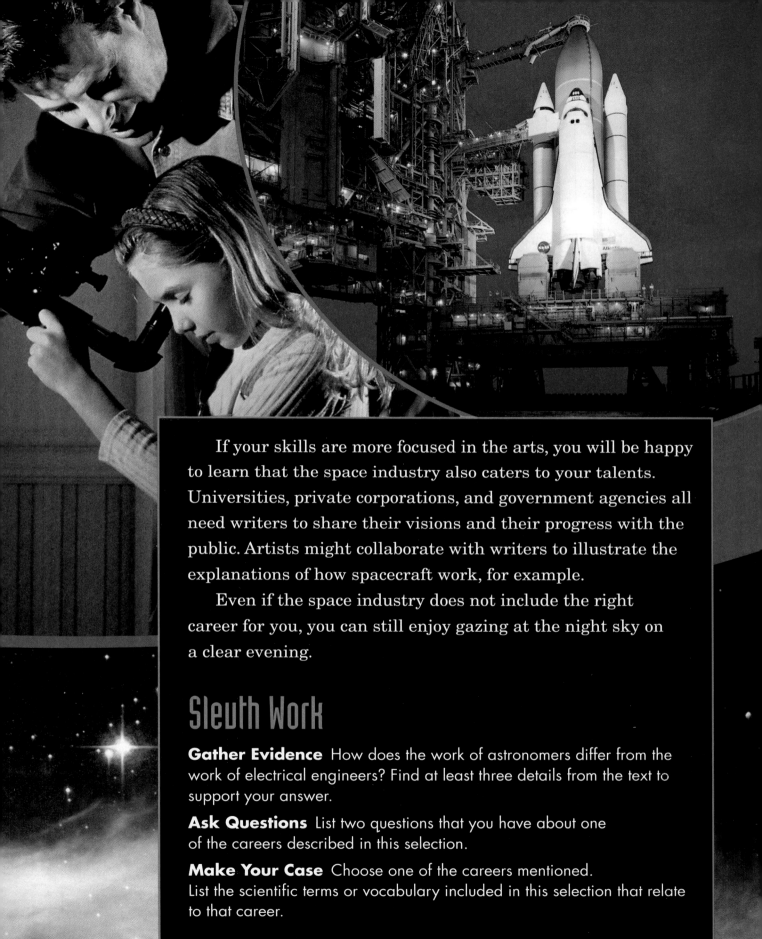

If your skills are more focused in the arts, you will be happy to learn that the space industry also caters to your talents. Universities, private corporations, and government agencies all need writers to share their visions and their progress with the public. Artists might collaborate with writers to illustrate the explanations of how spacecraft work, for example.

Even if the space industry does not include the right career for you, you can still enjoy gazing at the night sky on a clear evening.

Sleuth Work

Gather Evidence How does the work of astronomers differ from the work of electrical engineers? Find at least three details from the text to support your answer.

Ask Questions List two questions that you have about one of the careers described in this selection.

Make Your Case Choose one of the careers mentioned. List the scientific terms or vocabulary included in this selection that relate to that career.

Charlotte's Space Travel

Charlotte loved when her uncle visited. Uncle Ty was an engineer who worked for NASA (National Aeronautics and Space Administration). He told great stories about the rockets he helped design, and he often brought Charlotte books filled with beautiful photographs taken from space. She loved technology and science, and she was fairly adventurous. For those reasons, her family kept telling Charlotte she should be an astronaut when she grew up, but she just wasn't sure.

One Saturday, Charlotte and Uncle Ty took a trip to the city. They spent the day at the Museum of Natural History, which was hosting an exhibit on space travel. Uncle Ty provided a running narrative about various spacecraft and added interesting facts about the display of space suits and other astronaut gear. Charlotte was thrilled to try operating two model robot arms. These devices fascinated her.

By the time they got on the bus to return home, Charlotte was exhausted. Closing her eyes, she thought about what it would be like to zoom into space. As she drifted off to sleep, Charlotte started to feel the weightlessness astronauts must feel when they float in zero gravity. The next thing she knew, she was looking out the window not of a bus but of a space shuttle. She could see the vivid colors of Earth—brilliant blues and greens like she had never before witnessed.

Just then, one of her crew members floated over and nudged Charlotte, telling her she had to finish the task at hand quickly. Charlotte realized that she was maneuvering a giant robotic arm outside the space shuttle to tighten a loose panel. The pressure was on, and she felt nervous. But she kept at it. Soon enough the whole crew was celebrating Charlotte's success.

After a snack of granola, dried fruit, and nuts, the crew hooked their sleeping bags to the wall. They settled in for a good night's sleep after a long day. Charlotte dozed off, feeling proud of her accomplishment with the robotic arm and excited for the experiments they would set up the next day.

She felt like she had barely slept when all of a sudden she heard Uncle Ty's voice. "Wake up, Char," Uncle Ty whispered. "We're back home now." When Charlotte opened her eyes, she realized she had been dreaming, but this she knew for sure— she wanted to be an astronaut one day and couldn't wait for her first trip into space.

Sleuth Work

Gather Evidence What clues in the story suggest why Charlotte decides that she wants to be an astronaut when she grows up?

Ask Questions After reading, what three factual questions would you like to ask an astronaut about his or her experiences in space?

Make Your Case Compare and contrast Charlotte and her uncle. Cite information from the text in your answer.

MOVING TO MARS?

I was thinking last week about what it would be like if I moved to another planet. I see some advantages right away, of course. First, I might get my name into the history books as the First Resident in Space, which would be totally awesome. Second, it would be a great opportunity to get away from the bully down the street. And third, a planet like Mars has so little gravity that people can jump about three times higher there than they can on Earth. With a vertical leap like that, I'd be virtually unstoppable on the basketball court.

But I recognize downsides to the idea, too. For one thing, moving is a humongous hassle. Even if you just move across the state, you need to pack, say goodbye to neighbors, and take care of a lot of other stuff. Now imagine how much worse that would be if you were moving across the solar system. If you forget to pack even one thing, you might never see it again. And as for connecting with family and friends, I don't think you can rely on webcams on Mercury.

Then there's the little problem of always having to wear a space suit. Did you know that Earth is the only planet with enough oxygen to keep us alive? Temperatures are another big issue. It gets up to 460°C (860°F) on Venus—hot enough to fry not just an egg but also a person. As for Saturn, even the most powerful furnaces in the universe aren't going to keep you warm when it's around −178°C (−288°F) outdoors. I guess you'd probably live in a big dome so you could move around some, but not getting to go

Oh, and a lot of these planets are—well, let's just say that they're not like Earth. For instance, Jupiter consists mostly of gases like hydrogen and helium, so there isn't exactly anywhere to stand, let alone to play basketball. Venus has almost zero water, so can you imagine the cost of trying to ship some in from Earth? And the gusts on Neptune are almost ten times stronger than the winds we get here—good for extreme kite-flying, I guess, but not for much else.

So all in all, I plan on staying here on Earth if folks begin settling the other planets. Definitely. It's the only decision that makes any sense.

SLEUTH WORK

Gather Evidence List at least three facts about the solar system the writer uses to argue against the idea of moving to a new planet.

Ask Questions After reading the text, write three questions you would want to have answered about a planet before making a decision to move there.

Make Your Case Compare and contrast the narrator in this selection to Charlotte in the previous selection. Who do you think would make a better space traveler, and why?

Unit 4

Exploring New Worlds

Greetings, Sleuthhounds!

In this unit, you will be looking for clues about people who went on journeys. Here are some sleuth tips to help you. Good luck and have fun!

Sleuth Tips

Gather Evidence

How do sleuths remember clues?

- Sleuths might not remember everything. They take careful notes and write down details in case they forget.
- Sleuths find creative ways to keep track. They take notes, make lists, draw diagrams, and create charts.

Ask Questions

Why do sleuths ask questions?

- Sleuths use questions to help them gather more evidence. These questions can help them draw a conclusion.
- Sleuths think questioning can be wonderful and might lead to unexpected answers.

Make Your Case

How do sleuths disagree with other sleuths?

- Sleuths know that other sleuths might disagree. They understand the value in learning from others.
- Sleuths respect the conclusions of others. A super sleuth wants to find out how other sleuths used the evidence.

Prove It!

What do sleuths do before showing what they have learned?

- Sleuths remember to review the details in their notes, diagrams, and charts. They highlight what is most important.
- Sleuths want to persuade and convince others. They may write down key topics or use an outline.

A MAN OF PERSISTENCE

Explorer Sir Ernest Shackleton might be the most persistent man who ever lived. On December 5, 1914, he and twenty-seven men set out on a ship called *Endurance*. They hoped to reach the Antarctic continent and become the first people to cross the land on foot.

Despite the predictions of a terrible winter, *Endurance* left South Georgia Island, a remote island in the southern Atlantic Ocean. It headed for Vahsel Bay on Antarctica. Just two days later, the vessel ran into pack ice. For the next six weeks, the ship wove through ice floes.

On January 18, 1915, one day short of landing, the ship hit another thick pack ice. By the next morning, ice had enclosed the ship. Shackleton soon realized the ship was securely stuck in the ice and would remain stuck through many long winter months. During this time, Shackleton had his crew stick to their routines and exercise the sled dogs they had brought with them.

Ten months later, the crew still remained on board. In October 1915, pressure from the ice began to damage the ship, and it began slowly sinking. Shackleton and his crew abandoned the ship and made camp on the surrounding ice. On November 21, 1915, *Endurance* sank completely.

December 5, 1914 *Endurance* sets sail.	**January 18, 1915** *Endurance* stranded in ice.	**October 1915** Crew abandons ship.	**November 21, 1915** *Endurance* sinks.

The crew camped on the ice for several months, and in April 1916, the ice floe broke in half, causing the crew to flee in lifeboats. Days later, they landed on Elephant Island, about 350 miles from where the *Endurance* sank.

Shackleton knew he had to take a drastic step if they were ever to be rescued. Elephant Island was too remote for a rescue attempt. So a group of six men set off in a lifeboat for South Georgia Island, where their journey had begun.

The lifeboat landed on the west side of South Georgia Island in May 1916. The whaling stations—the only source of rescue—were on the east side. Shackleton and two others left on foot to travel the twenty-two miles to the nearest stations.

Within thirty-six hours, the men had made it to a whaling station and began planning the crew's rescue. Finally, on August 30, 1916, the crew was rescued from Elephant Island. After almost two years, the ordeal was over, and not one crew member had died. It was an amazing expedition with a happy ending because of one man's persistence to bring everyone home.

SLEUTH WORK

Gather Evidence Shackleton was a persistent man. Write three details from the text that support this statement.

Ask Questions If you could talk to Sir Shackleton about the decisions he made, what three questions would you ask?

Make Your Case The writer states that this was an "amazing expedition." What support is provided for that statement?

April 1916
Crew flees in lifeboats. Some settle on Elephant Island. Others head to South Georgia Island to get help.

May 1916
Small crew lands on South Georgia Island.

August 30, 1916
All crew members rescued from Elephant Island.

Pants with History

Did you know those denim pants you see everywhere are part of American history? This is the story of how two hardworking and creative immigrants came together to produce the first blue jeans.

In 1848, a young German named Loeb Strauss immigrated to New York with his mother and two sisters. His older brothers owned a company that sold fabric and clothing there. After gold was discovered in California, Strauss saw it as a business opportunity. Gold was a valuable resource. Some gold prospectors "struck it rich." Many other people grew wealthy providing the more mundane goods and services to the miners and other California settlers. In 1853, young Strauss, now called Levi, traveled to California. He began distributing his brothers' fabric and clothing.

Contrary to popular myth, however, Levi Strauss did not invent the blue jeans known as "Levi's." Born in Latvia (LAT-vee-uh), Jacob Davis was a tailor who made clothing. He also made items like horse blankets. The demand for heavy-duty work clothes grew. Davis, who lived in Nevada, began making "waist-high overalls" from cotton duck fabric, which is like canvas. He purchased the cotton duck from Strauss. The term *blue jeans* comes from a fabric called "jean." It is much like denim and was used to make pants in the nineteenth century.

Levi Strauss

Because thread alone wasn't strong enough to fasten the pockets onto the pants, Jacob decided to add copper rivets. He had successfully used rivets on horse blankets. As the durable pants became more popular with miners, ranchers, and farmers, Davis decided to obtain a patent. In 1872, he wrote to Strauss. He offered to share the rights to the riveting process if Strauss would help mass market the product.

Strauss then brought Davis to San Francisco to supervise the manufacture of riveted jeans by Levi Strauss & Co. On May 20, 1873, the patent was granted. That day is considered the official birthday of blue jeans. The pants soon became a best seller. Straus and Davis had struck "blue gold."

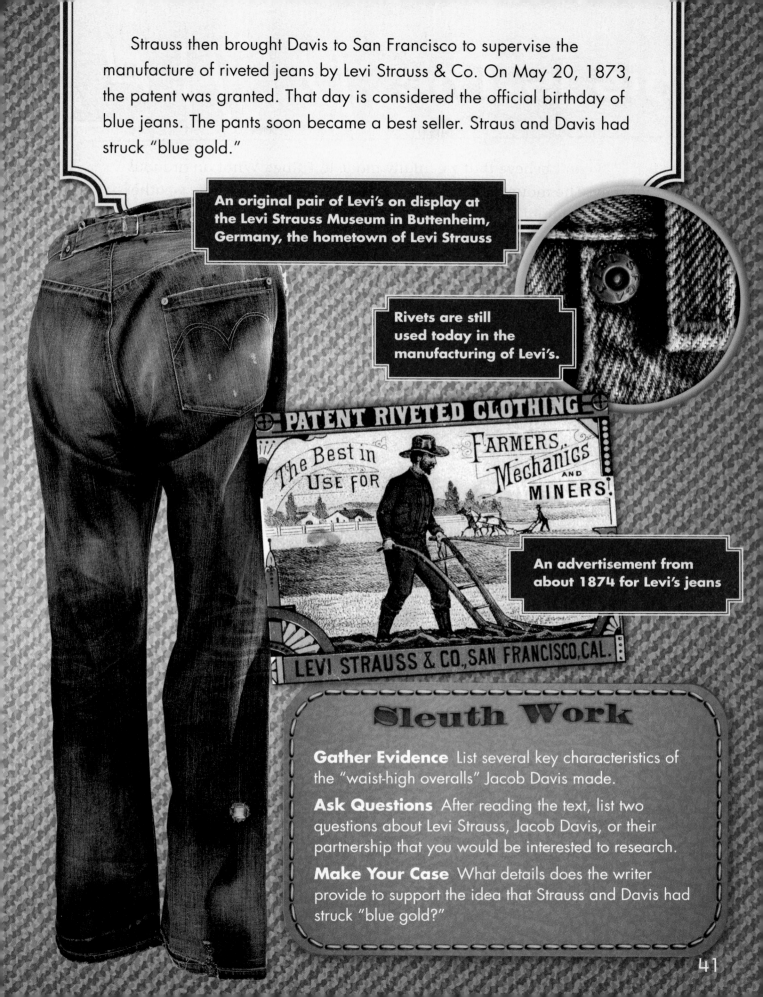

An original pair of Levi's on display at the Levi Strauss Museum in Buttenheim, Germany, the hometown of Levi Strauss

Rivets are still used today in the manufacturing of Levi's.

PATENT RIVETED CLOTHING

The Best in USE FOR

FARMERS, Mechanics AND MINERS!

LEVI STRAUSS & CO., SAN FRANCISCO, CAL.

An advertisement from about 1874 for Levi's jeans

Sleuth Work

Gather Evidence List several key characteristics of the "waist-high overalls" Jacob Davis made.

Ask Questions After reading the text, list two questions about Levi Strauss, Jacob Davis, or their partnership that you would be interested to research.

Make Your Case What details does the writer provide to support the idea that Strauss and Davis had struck "blue gold?"

This Is The PLACE

"I can't believe that we finally made it, Father. What an arduous journey! The mountains, the rivers, the buffalo herds, and the weather—I've had enough!" exclaimed Rebecca.

"Indeed, Rebecca. We have endured many hardships, but seeing this great expanse of land and knowing that our pioneer brothers and sisters are here I feel relieved."

Rebecca and her family had traveled for months, along with hundreds of other Mormons, to the Salt Lake Valley. They had no idea that the first Mormon settlement, in Nauvoo, Illinois, would not be permanent.

Rebecca sighed, and wrapped her arms around her twin sisters. "At least we are together and no one perished." She looked all around and breathed in the clear, cleansing air. "This land seems so peaceful and safe unlike Nauvoo. I just hope this valley does not bring us the same circumstances. It was so unfair how people treated us there!" Rebecca cried, and abruptly sat down on a rock.

"We may always feel persecuted, Rebecca, you must understand that. This is why Brigham Young has led us west, far away from other settlements, so that we can worship freely—and without human judgment," explained her father.

"I wonder how Mr. Young knew that this valley would be a safe haven for us?" wondered Rebecca. She rose from the rock and squinted at the blazing sun.

"He is a wise man, a true follower of the faith, and a fearless leader, Rebecca. When he arrived here, Young said, 'This is the place, drive on'," added her father.

Rebecca replied, "I am thankful, Papa, that we have a new home and a place to practice our religion and way of life without being ridiculed, yet I do miss our home back east. I yearn to see my friends and my school."

Rebecca's father shook his head and approached Rebecca. "I understand, but your school and your friends' families, all of them thought of you differently because you are Mormon."

"You're right, Papa," but it's just not fair. How could our countrymen, who came to this land to seek religious freedom, practice such hypocrisy?" argued Rebecca. Rebecca stomped away, kicking dirt with her tattered boot to release some aggression. She sat down on the back of the wagon to gather her thoughts. Her father pushed a wooden chest out of the way and sat next to her. He wiped Rebecca's hair away from her weary face and prayed.

BE A SLEUTH

Gather Evidence Using evidence in the text, explain why Rebecca and her family were moving.

Ask Questions After reading the text, write one question you would ask a historian about this time period and one question you would ask Rebecca's father.

Make Your Case Compare and contrast the life the family was leaving behind to the life the family expected in the Salt Lake Valley.

Making a Difference for Immigrants

John Michael Kohler

People have been immigrating to America for hundreds of years. They have come for adventure, wealth, work opportunities, and to escape persecution. Often that's what they have found. They also often found themselves in unfamiliar surroundings and among people who didn't want them here. One inspiring company went out of its way to make life better for immigrants.

In the late nineteenth century, young John Michael Kohler immigrated to the United States from Austria with his family. Kohler grew up and married a woman whose father co-owned a successful business in the steel and iron works industry. Kohler then purchased the business from his father-in-law in 1873, and the Kohler Company was founded. The company soon manufactured bathtubs and bath fixtures near Sheboygan, Wisconsin, and continues to do so today.

Kohler needed a great many workers to make all those bathtubs, sinks, and toilets! Unlike many other companies of that time, which exploited immigrants for labor, the Kohler Company tried to provide a better life for its employees.

Village of Kohler, Wisconsin

Kohler Company workers, 1889

Walter Kohler

Many of Kohler's workers were Austrian immigrants, just like John Michael Kohler was. The company emphasized worker safety, medical care, and good wages. One of the company's priorities was to ensure that Kohler employees not only had pleasant working conditions but also decent living conditions. Kohler began transforming the Village of Kohler into one of the first planned communities in the Midwest. The town had many attractive features: green spaces, single and two-family homes, recreational facilities, and a school. Creating a company town helped the Kohler business attract and keep a stable workforce.

The Kohler Company still wanted to do more so it built the American Club, a dormitory for immigrant employees. Housing costs were minimal. Many unmarried Kohler employees stayed there until they saved enough to buy a house and send for their families. Employees took lessons in English, American history, and civics. Immigrant workers got a day off and transportation to the courthouse as a first step toward becoming citizens. Between 1900 and 1930, the Kohler Company helped at least 1,200 immigrant workers become citizens.

Immigrants may have very different reasons for coming here, but most arrive with high hopes. The Kohler Company made a difference in the lives of its immigrant workers who were trying to make a new and better life in a foreign land.

Sleuth Work

Gather Evidence What evidence can you find to explain why John Michael Kohler wanted to help immigrants who worked for his company?

Ask Questions After reading the text, what questions about the Village of Kohler or the American Club would you like to research further?

Make Your Case Summarize the opinion the writer expresses. Find at least three details the writer uses to support that opinion.

Acknowledgments

Photographs

Every effort has been made to secure permission and provide appropriate credit for photographic material. The publisher deeply regrets any omission and pledges to correct errors called to its attention in subsequent editions.

Unless otherwise acknowledged, all photographs are the property of Pearson Education, Inc.

Photo locators denoted as follows: Top (T), Center (C), Bottom (B), Left (L), Right (R), Background (Bkgd)

Cover Chandler Digital Art

4 (Bkgd) Nightman/Fotolia, (T) dimedrol/Fotolia, (C) Shutterstock, (Bkgd) bejim/Fotolia, (BR) taelove/Shutterstock; **5** (C) tungphoto/Fotolia, (TR) phant/Fotolia, (BC) hljdesign/Fotolia, (BR) Maxx-Studio/Shutterstock; **8** (Bkgd) Hemera Technologies/Thinkstock, (T) Thinkstock/Hemera Technologies, (C) TFoxFoto/Shutterstock, (B) Rigucci/Shutterstock; **10** (Bkgd) Jupiterimages/Thinkstock, (TL) akhug/Fotolia, (B) DelmasLehman/Fotolia, (TR) Joseph Scott/Fotolia, (BR) HeikoKiera/Fotolia; **11** (Bkgd) Jupiterimages/Thinkstock, (TR) Davy HILLER/Fotolia, (CR) Paul/Fotolia; **12** (TR) Comstock/Thinkstock, (CR) Tammy Venable/Fotolia, (BR) Stockbyte/Thinkstock, (Bkgd) sumnersgraphicsinc/Fotolia; **13** Eric Isselée/Fotolia; **14** Library of Congress; **15** Organica/Alamy; **18** (Bkgd) Mates/Fotolia, (C) David M Schrader/Fotolia, (CR) IMagine/Fotolia, (BR) Thinkstock, (TL) Library of Congress; **19** Lacabetyar/Fotolia; **20** (BL) Jorge Salcedo/Shutterstock, (BR) Dorling Kindersley Ltd, (C) Luminis/Fotolia, LLC, (Bkgd) Library of Congress; **21** Dorling Kindersley Ltd; **22** (Bkgd) Ryan McVay/Thinkstock, (C) Everett Collection/Alamy; **23** HABS or HAER or HALS/Library of Congress; **24** (Bkgd) Natis/Fotolia, (B) Thinkstock, (TL) Library of Congress; **28** (TR) sco122/Fotolia, (Bkgd) Strezhnev Pavel/Fotolia; **29** Jeff Rotman/Alamy; **30** (TR) Ablestock/Thinkstock, (B) NASA; **31** Bill Ingalls/NASA; **32** (Bkgd) marcel/Fotolia; **32** (CR) Kovalenko Inna/Fotolia; **33** NASA; **34** (TL) picsfive/Fotolia, (CR) Henrik Lehnerer/Shutterstock; **35** (CL) Arunas Gabalis/Fotolia, (CR) Dorling Kindersley Ltd, (Bkgd) NASA; **38** (T) SSilver/Fotolia, (BR) UK History/Alamy, (TR) Library of Congress; **40** Pictorial Press Ltd/Alamy; **41** (L) A369 Daniel Karmann Deutsche Presse-Agentur/Newscom, (CR) Pictorial Press Ltd/Alamy, (TR) Karmousha/Fotolia; **42** John Schupbach/Fotolia; **44** (Bkgd) Ryan McVay/Thinkstock, (CR, CL, B) Kohler Co.; **45** Kohler Co.